THIS BOOK BELONGS TO:

....

....

BY MOOREA SEAL

JOURNALS

The 52 Lists Project

52 Lists for Happiness

52 Lists for Togetherness

52 Lists for Calm

52 Lists for Bravery

STATIONERY

52 Lists Planner

52 Lists Postcards

52 Lists "My Weekly List" Desk Pad

52 Lists "To Do List" Notepad

BOOKS

Make Yourself at Home

52 Lists
for
Bravery

JOURNALING INSPIRATION
for COURAGE, RESILIENCE,
and INNER STRENGTH

BY MOOREA SEAL

SASQUATCH BOOKS
SEATTLE

52 Lists
for
Bravery

JOURNALING INSPIRATION
for COURAGE, RESILIENCE,
and INNER STRENGTH

BY MOOREA SEAL

SASQUATCH BOOKS
SEATTLE

To the self that has yet to find space to exist. To the voice waiting to speak: the inner poet, the maker, the scientist, the musician, the philosopher, the researcher, the painter, the self-expressionist, the list maker . . .

As you seek that which inspires you, may you find the bravery to turn your inspiration into actualization.

I have always been curious why some people are able to push through challenges more easily than others. Through years of researching thinkers, educators, and activists, I've come to find one thing to be true. It is through the challenging things that happen to us (and the challenges we create knowingly or unknowingly for ourselves) that we gain the opportunity to build our bravery. Of course we want to have easy, peaceful lives. But without facing struggles, we do not have the opportunity to overcome. The most inspirational people in the world do not become so by avoiding what scares them. Instead, they pursue being true to themselves amidst the things that, at first look, appear to hold them back. You also have the chance to transform your challenges into your greatest sources of strength. Yes, even the scary stuff! That said, it is important to be aware of privilege and how it plays a role in the ability to speak up and stand up, for yourself and others. In a culture that is set up to value whiteness, maleness, heterosexuality, wealth, and ability (among other attributes), we tend to celebrate people with privilege when they speak up, while people without those privileges are second-guessed or stereotyped. The same acts of bravery carry different levels of risk for different people. Be aware of the power and privileges you do have, and consider how you can support and empower not just yourself, but everyone around you. With the list prompts in this book, you'll find easy, accessible, and fun ways to build your bravery, gain resilience, and truly face the challenges of your life with a deeper belief in yourself. May you find what you seek as your words fill each list. I hope your voice grows louder with my belief in your ability to rise up.

xo Moorea Seal

Get Together

There is a warrior within you just waiting to come out. With each list you complete, you are one step closer to expressing that inner warrior. There are so many people on this same journey; you're not alone. Join this brave community! Use the hashtag **#52ListsforBravery** when posting about your lists on social media, and explore other posts to see the insights people are gathering from their list making. The insights you share may help others on their journeys toward bravery as well. Your vulnerability is a source of empowerment, not just for yourself, but for those who encounter it. When you share your experiences, you are inspiring countless others. And you might just find inspiration from others to uplift you too in your own journey to a braver life.

———————————

Learn more about the 52 Lists series at
MooreaSeal.com/pages/52Lists.

Other hashtags to explore:
**#52ListsProject | #52Lists | #52HappyLists
#52ListsforHappiness | #52ListsforTogetherness
#52ListsforCalm**

Contents

Dream

Dedicate

Step Up

Rise Up

Dream

Tell me, what is it you plan to do
with your one wild and precious life?

—MARY OLIVER

Everyone has a starting point, a challenge that must be faced to wake up the warrior within. What is your challenge? What is it that *you* want to be brave for? Whether there is an external force outside of you that requires bravery (whether you want to or not) or there are things you've known you need to change but haven't had the guts to tackle yet, this book is for you. You deserve to know that not only can you survive, but you can also have the space to dream, the opportunity to plan, and the freedom and strength to rise to any occasion.

Now is the time to dream big, to let go of the boundaries you think hold you in. In the pages ahead, you will have the opportunity to discover the voice inside that says *I can and I will*. Each list in the sections ahead is crafted to help you discover and clarify your big dreams. Perhaps you need to change your career path, move somewhere new, let go of an unhealthy relationship, or gather the strength to try something you've never attempted (or succeeded at) before. You *are* strong enough, and your source of bravery already lives within you. Let's uncover it by dreaming big.

List 1

LIST THE WORDS YOU ASSOCIATE WITH BRAVERY.

....

....

....

....

....

....

....

....

....

....

....

....

....

....

_____

_____

_____

_____

_____

_____

_____

_____

_____

_____

_____

_____

_____

TAKE ACTION: In a place you spend a lot of time (at home or work), dedicate an object or hang a note or affirmation to remind you that bravery is always within arm's reach if you seek it.

List 2

LIST THE ISSUES, STRUGGLES, AND CHALLENGES
WITHIN YOURSELF THAT YOU WANT TO BUILD THE
BRAVERY TO TACKLE OR FACE.

....

....

....

....

....

....

....

....

....

....

....

....

TAKE ACTION: These are the things that are within your control. And these are the things that, if you are willing to accept or change them, will become your tools for facing your external challenges. Star the things you want to change, and underline the things you would like to learn to accept as they are, even if it feels impossible.

List 3

LIST THE PEOPLE, SITUATIONS, AND ISSUES *OUTSIDE OF YOURSELF* THAT YOU WOULD LIKE TO BUILD THE BRAVERY TO TACKLE OR FACE.

....

....

....

....

....

TAKE ACTION: It's a whole lot easier to accept or change the external once you have worked on your inner needs and owned them. For the rest of the Dream section of this journal, put these external issues to the side so that you can first focus on your internal self. Choose one phrase to motivate yourself to pursue acceptance:

I WILL TRY, AND TRY AGAIN.

I AM SCARED, BUT I WILL DO MY BEST.

I GIVE MYSELF PERMISSION TO SET THESE THINGS ASIDE FOR NOW.

List 4

LIST THE PEOPLE/ANIMALS YOU'VE CARED FOR, THE GOOD
YOU'VE DONE, AND THE THINGS YOU HAVE ACCOMPLISHED
THAT MAKE YOU FEEL GOOD ABOUT YOURSELF.

TAKE ACTION: Write a letter to someone who supported you in the good you have pursued. Tell them how they helped you and how it makes you feel to push through fear to seek kindness, empathy, and empowerment.

List 5

LIST THE WAYS YOU WANT TO GROW AND
IMPROVE AS A PERSON: EMOTIONALLY,
INTELLECTUALLY, SPIRITUALLY, AND PHYSICALLY.

....

....

....

....

....

....

....

....

....

....

....

....

TAKE ACTION: There is a difference between aspiring to be something and actually expecting yourself to be something. Now is the time to be truthful about the expectations you set for yourself. Choose one thing from this list and put a star next to it, marking it as the *one* thing you expect yourself to become better at this year.

List 6

LIST THE THINGS YOU VISUALIZE HAVING, DOING,
AND BEING IN YOUR DREAM LIFE.

···

···

···

···

···

···

···

···

···

···

···

···

TAKE ACTION: Next to each of the things that you don't have in your life currently, write "not yet." Because that is the truth. You have time. You may not have the things you want and need right now, but in life, you have the chance to pursue that which you need and want—if not now, soon—with bravery. You are *never* a failure if you allow yourself to try again.

List 7

LIST THE THINGS YOU ONCE DREAMT OF HAVING IN
YOUR LIFE THAT YOU *DO* HAVE NOW.

....

....

....

....

....

....

....

....

....

....

....

....

TAKE ACTION: How did each of these things come into being? Underline the things that required bravery to attain.

List 8

LIST THE TIMES HOPE HAS HELPED YOU THROUGH
AN EXPERIENCE OR SITUATION.

....

....

....

....

....

....

....

....

....

....

....

TAKE ACTION: Hope is essential to being brave. If we lose hope, we lose belief in our abilities. The next time you are feeling down and lacking in motivation, turn to this page and reread how hope has helped you in the past. Let it remind you that hope is always there for you and that when you tap into it, your bravery grows.

The future belongs to those who believe in the beauty of their dreams.

—ELEANOR ROOSEVELT

List 9

LIST WHAT YOU NEED IN YOUR LIFE RIGHT NOW.

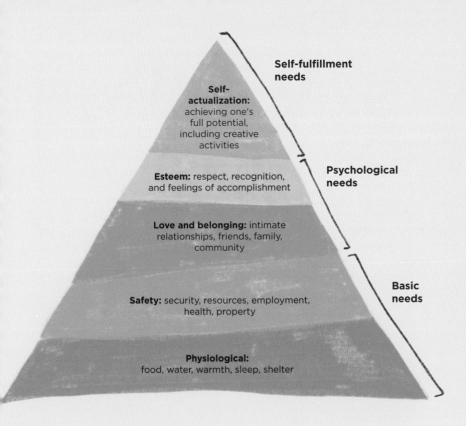

Self-fulfillment needs

Self-actualization: achieving one's full potential, including creative activities

Psychological needs

Esteem: respect, recognition, and feelings of accomplishment

Love and belonging: intimate relationships, friends, family, community

Basic needs

Safety: security, resources, employment, health, property

Physiological: food, water, warmth, sleep, shelter

TAKE ACTION: We all have needs, and one simple thing that fulfills a need is better than nothing. Having a sip of water is better than no water. But a full glass of water is even more fulfilling, healing, and relieving.

Look at psychologist Abraham Maslow's Hierarchy of Needs above. What is one thing you really need more of right now?

....

What will you do this week to manifest this in your life?

List 10

LIST THE DREAMS YOU HAVE FOR OTHERS.

....

....

....

....

....

....

....

....

....

TAKE ACTION: It's important to know that we have no control over what the people we love do with their lives, though we are allowed to hold hopes and dreams for them. Instead of seeking to control how others live, meditate on the word *empowerment*. How can you create resources for the people you love to pursue *their* dreams? When you seek to provide ways for others to grow in their own needs and desires, you are showing the deepest love they will ever know.

List 11

LIST THE FICTIONAL HEROES YOU ADMIRE.

....

....

....

....

....

....

....

....

....

....

....

TAKE ACTION: Next to each of their names, write down qualities of their character that you would like to emulate. Is there a certain word that stands out the most to you? Write it here:

....

Let this be your personal mantra for the week ahead.

List 12

LIST THE REAL-LIFE PEOPLE WHOM YOU ADMIRE
FOR THEIR BRAVERY.

··

··

··

··

··

··

··

··

··

··

TAKE ACTION: Send one of these people a note expressing your admiration for how their bravery has cultivated a better life for themselves and those around them, and share what you hope to learn from them.

List 13

LIST THE PLACES AROUND YOUR HOME, WORK SPACE,
OR NEIGHBORHOOD THAT MAKE YOU FEEL REFRESHED,
INSPIRED, MOTIVATED, AND FOCUSED.

....

....

....

....

....

....

....

....

....

TAKE ACTION: The spaces we occupy have a *huge* impact on how we feel about ourselves and can even reflect our emotional and intellectual state. It's easy to get comfortable and settled in the same routines and the same physical spaces, but we can promote bravery just by stepping outside of our routine and spicing things up, whether you step out emotionally, intellectually, or physically. Choose a new place to work on your next list, to encourage you to dedicate yourself to bravery.

Dedicate

Life shrinks or expands in proportion
to one's courage.

—ANAÏS NIN

Let's get motivated! It's time to get focused on making your dreams a reality. When you finally allow yourself to see all the ways that you have the potential to grow, your courage might feel a little shaky, but there is no need to let fear stop you from moving forward. Within each list is a new way to bolster your bravery to turn dreams into realities, and it all begins with dedication. You are already building resilience and empowerment to envision a bolder, braver life. The future holds no bounds on the person that you can and will be. It begins with seeing the potential within you, which you have collected and put to paper in your previous lists. Let's move forward, transforming your dreams into motivators, realities that can be manifested through taking steps, one at a time, on the path to the future you dream of.

List 14

WHAT FEARS OR PAST EXPERIENCES DO
YOU HOLD THAT FEEL LIKE BLOCKADES TO
MANIFESTING YOUR DREAMS?

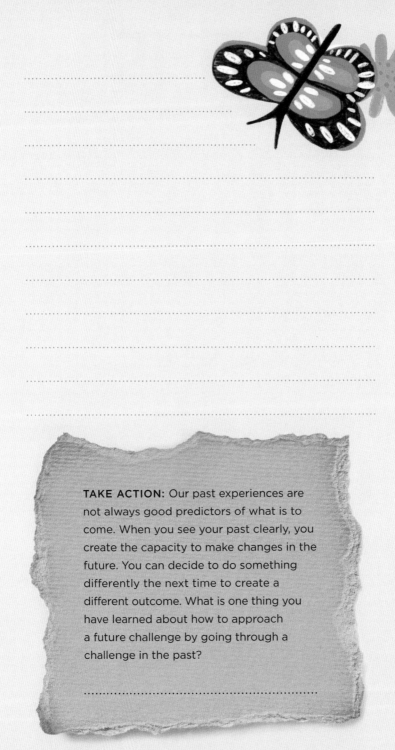

....

....

....

....

....

....

....

....

....

....

TAKE ACTION: Our past experiences are not always good predictors of what is to come. When you see your past clearly, you create the capacity to make changes in the future. You can decide to do something differently the next time to create a different outcome. What is one thing you have learned about how to approach a future challenge by going through a challenge in the past?

....

List 15

LIST THE SITUATIONS WHERE YOU COULD TAKE
MORE EMOTIONAL RISKS AND THE PEOPLE YOU
COULD TAKE SUCH RISKS WITH.

- [ ] ....
- [ ] ....
- [ ] ....
- [ ] ....
- [ ] ....
- [ ] ....
- [ ] ....
- [ ] ....
- [ ] ....
- [ ] ....
- [ ] ....
- [ ] ....
- [ ] ....

- ☐ ....
- ☐ ....
- ☐ ....
- ☐ ....
- ☐ ....
- ☐ ....
- ☐ ....
- ☐ ....
- ☐ ....
- ☐ ....

TAKE ACTION: Using a scale of 1 (totally terrified) to 10 (totally comfortable), write a number next to each person and situation, marking how comfortable you feel taking an emotional risk in that area. Next, circle at least one person/situation where you are willing to try to take a risk and be more emotionally open at your next opportunity. This is where your bravery can take action and grow.

List 16

LIST THE THINGS THAT MAKE YOU FEEL STRONG:
EMOTIONALLY, PHYSICALLY, INTELLECTUALLY,
AND SPIRITUALLY.

....

....

....

....

....

....

....

....

....

....

....

TAKE ACTION: Circle the thing that feels most powerful and easiest to access as a source of strength. Make a note of this somewhere that you reference often, be it in your calendar, on your phone, or on a note next to your bed, so you can always remember: you have resources for strength at your fingertips.

List 17

LIST THE ASSETS IN YOUR LIFE THAT YOU WOULD BENEFIT
FROM INVESTING MORE TIME INTO, WHETHER IT BE PEOPLE,
PHYSICAL RESOURCES, ACTIVITIES, OR SKILLS.

....

....

....

....

....

....

....

....

....

....

....

....

TAKE ACTION: Circle the easiest thing you could invest in this week. Once you pursue it, write down here what you feel you gained from redirecting attention to something you already have.

List 18

LIST THE SITUATIONS IN WHICH YOU HAVE
FELT BRAVEST IN THE PAST.

....

....

....

....

....

....

....

....

....

....

....

....

....

....

....

....

....

....

....

....

....

....

....

TAKE ACTION: What sorts of results did you get from being brave? Write one example of how bravery helped you achieve or receive something you wanted.

List 19

LIST THE WAYS YOU PHYSICALLY
FEEL SHAME AND/OR GUILT.

....

....

....

....

....

....

....

....

....

....

....

....

....

....

TAKE ACTION: Circle where shame and guilt feel tied to your body, whether you feel shame about your physical self or feel like shame sits in a certain area of your body when you feel it emotionally. Take a moment each morning to put your hands, or just your mind, on this part of your body and say to yourself, "I deserve acceptance and love. I accept myself. I love myself." Acceptance takes practice; it's OK if it feels false at first. Keep going until it starts to feel true.

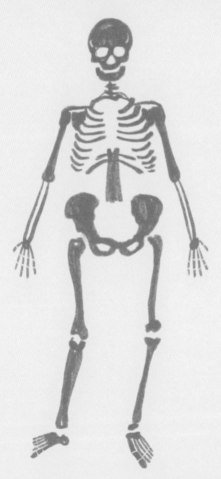

Courage is the most important of all the virtues because without courage, you can't practice any other virtue consistently.

—MAYA ANGELOU

List 20

WHAT IS ONE PROBLEM OR CHALLENGE YOU CURRENTLY HAVE IN YOUR LIFE? LIST ALL THE POSSIBLE REACTIONS YOU COULD HAVE TO THIS CHALLENGE.

....

....

....

....

....

....

....

....

....

....

....

....

TAKE ACTION: Underline the answers that show you engaging with a problem and facing it, versus the answers that show you turning away or ignoring the problem. You build resilience each time you face a problem, which gives you more bravery because you have evidence that you can handle challenges.

List 21

LIST THE PEOPLE YOU COMPARE YOURSELF TO.

....

....

....

....

....

....

....

TAKE ACTION: Next to each person's name, write the emotion you typically feel when comparing yourself to them. How can you reframe how you view each person, from comparing to feeling empowered by observing the incredible people they are? Other people's successes have no negative impact on the person you are. Every person's life is unique, and every person you admire has secret struggles and advantages you may never know about. Transform their achievements into your own inspiration and self-empowerment.

List 22

LIST THE THINGS THAT MAKE YOU FEEL
COMFORTABLE AND SECURE.

....

....

....

....

....

....

....

....

....

....

TAKE ACTION: Building security and comfort in your life is vital in feeling stable and capable. And to cultivate *more* sources of security in your life, you must step outside of your current comfort zone on occasion. When you do, you have the chance to build a new source of comfort and resilience in your life because you faced it! What is one way you will seek to step outside of your comfort zone this week?

List 23

LIST THE THINGS YOU ONLY WANT TO DO IF THEY
CAN BE DONE PERFECTLY.

....

....

....

....

....

....

....

....

....

....

TAKE ACTION: The fact is, we often have to try something multiple times to get anywhere close to doing it well. Perseverance is more valuable than talent. Remember that. Some estimate that it takes ten thousand hours of practice to master something, and while inherent talent does make it easier, no one is talented in every area of life. What is one thing you are willing to put time and effort into, even if you never reach perfection?

List 24

LIST THE TIMES YOU HAVE HAD TO DISAPPOINT SOMEONE
TO DO WHAT YOU BELIEVED WAS RIGHT FOR YOU.

....

....

....

....

....

....

....

....

....

....

....

....

....

TAKE ACTION: One of the bravest acts is to follow your gut and do what you believe is right for you, even when someone you love may disagree. Who is one person whom you feel you have disappointed in the past, but who is still in your life and shows you they love you in their own unique ways?

List 25

LIST THE THINGS FROM YOUR CHILDHOOD THAT
FELT LIKE A CHALLENGE AT THE TIME BUT ARE NOW
EASY PARTS OF YOUR LIFE.

TAKE ACTION: From learning to tie your shoes to learning to read and write, there are so many ways that kids must choose bravery daily to persevere through something they have never done before. You are still that same child inside. If little you could learn and adapt to new experiences, grown-up you can too. This week, channel the wonder of a child and seek out a new experience without worrying about the outcome. No pressure, no need to become an expert overnight. Just try something!

One new experience I will seek out this week:

....

List 26

LIST THE LOFTIEST GOALS YOU CAN THINK OF—
THE DREAMS THAT FEEL LIKE THEY HAVE NO
CHANCE OF COMING TRUE.

A BEACHY PLACE TO STAY FOR THE WINTERS
SOMEWHERE WARM & SUNNY, GREEN & LUSH
THAT WE STAY FOR WINTERS. THE FREEDOM
FROM WORK, BILLS, ETC TO GO & BE THERE.
WE DON'T LEAVE UNTIL AFTER CHRISTMAS
THOUGH, MAYBE EVEN NEW YEARS - SO WE
CAN FULLY INDULGE IN THE CHRISTMAS
SEASON. SOMETIMES OUR FAMILIES VISIT
AND STAY c̄ US FOR A BIT. OUR KIDS
KEEP UP c̄ SCHOOL REMOTELY & ATTEND
SOME SORT OF EDUCATIONAL / OUTDOORS
PROGRAM WHILE WE ARE THERE. EVERY DAY
HAS SWIMMING, WALKING, BIKING, SNORKELING,

....

....

....

....

....

....

....

....

....

....

....

TAKE ACTION: It's not humility that holds us back; it's doubt in our own ability to rise to a seemingly impossible occasion. And representation matters in helping each of us believe we can get somewhere, or achieve something that seems unattainable to us. But when there is a lack of visible trailblazers who reflect ourselves, it means *you* could be that first one. Look out a window each morning this week and say this: I AM THE FIRST.

Step Up

Forever—is composed of Nows.

—EMILY DICKINSON

There truly is no time like the present. Our lives move forward as the clock spins, whether we wish it were so or not. And because of this, we have so many opportunities to practice living in the moment. With each step forward, each misstep or mistake, each reroute or newly open pathway, we have a chance to practice living boldly. Even the hard stuff that feels like a blockade in our path is teaching us something. And you and I are not the first to realize and own this truth. Our ancestors lived side by side with giant ferocious animals, foraging and hunting, providing for generations to come; their bravery is obvious because they had no other choice but to keep going, to navigate their wild environments, to survive, and live. We are all descended from those brave ancestors.

In today's age, it's the mental and emotional challenges that we more often have to face, in our relationships, in places of work and education, and in society at large. We cannot escape the things that happen *to* us, though we can control what we choose to pursue. And it is because of this that the courage to keep going is imperative for our own survival, emotionally, mentally, physically, and spiritually. It's time to step up, to put what you have been working on into action! May the lists waiting for you in the pages to come be anchors of bravery and bolsters of your inner confidence to prevail through whatever challenges you may face in life. Self-empowerment is available to you: the ability to face your fears and not just cope with them, but actually accept and move past them. Step up to the plate, and let's practice bravery.

List 27

LIST THE OCCASIONS WHEN YOU DECIDED TO BE
BRAVE ON BEHALF OF SOMEONE ELSE.

TAKE ACTION: Is it easier for you to be brave on behalf of others rather than yourself? The next time you need to be brave for yourself, imagine you are being brave on behalf of someone you love. Let this list remind you that *you* deserve to love, believe in, and advocate for yourself as much as you do for others.

List 28

LIST THE ANIMALS, BOTH REAL-LIFE CREATURES AND
THE FANTASTICAL, THAT REPRESENT BRAVERY TO YOU.

....

....

....

....

....

....

....

....

....

....

....

....

TAKE ACTION: Next to each creature, write down how they exhibit bravery. Underline the one you feel most inspired by. Next time you need to draw on bravery, imagine yourself as that animal.

List 29

LIST THE THINGS THAT FELT BLACK AND WHITE WHEN
YOU WERE YOUNGER BUT FEEL MORE GRAY TODAY.

TAKE ACTION: draw a symbol of growth and letting go—a tree, a bird, whatever elicits your understanding of finding ease in your emotions and opinions.

List 30

ASK YOUR FRIENDS AND FAMILY: WHAT IS
ONE INSTANCE IN THEIR PAST WHEN THEY
CHOSE TO BE BRAVE AND FACE SOMETHING
CHALLENGING? LIST OUT THEIR ANSWERS.

....

....

....

....

....

....

....

....

....

....

....

TAKE ACTION: Ask your loved ones follow-up questions: What is one way you want to be braver in your life right now? How do your past experiences make you feel capable of facing challenges in the present?

List 31

LIST THE CRITICISMS YOU'VE RECEIVED IN THE PAST THAT
HAVE HELPED YOU TO BECOME A BETTER YOU.

....

....

....

....

....

....

....

....

....

....

TAKE ACTION: Allowing criticism to exist in your life is one of the greatest markers of bravery. You can and will bounce back from critique *if* you decide to give yourself the chance to practice receiving it (especially when it hurts). The next time you hear criticism from someone, follow these steps: 1. Respond with "Thanks for the feedback." 2. Take time to process your feelings, either alone or with someone else, whichever feels easier. 3. Decide what percentage of their feedback you want to take, and use it to your advantage. Then let go of whatever feels like it isn't needed for your personal growth.

List 32

LIST THE THINGS ABOUT YOURSELF THAT YOU
THINK ARE SILLY, GOOFY, AND FUNNY.

....

....

....

....

....

....

....

....

....

....

....

....

TAKE ACTION: Which of these things do you think are embarrassing to share with someone you love? This week's challenge is to move past the embarrassment and get silly! Sometimes it takes a little bravery to let your hair down and get goofy. Laughter is such a great healer and stress reliever, so go ahead—get funny.

List 33

LIST THE LABELS PEOPLE HAVE GIVEN YOU AND
THE WAYS THEY HAVE TRIED TO BOX YOU IN.

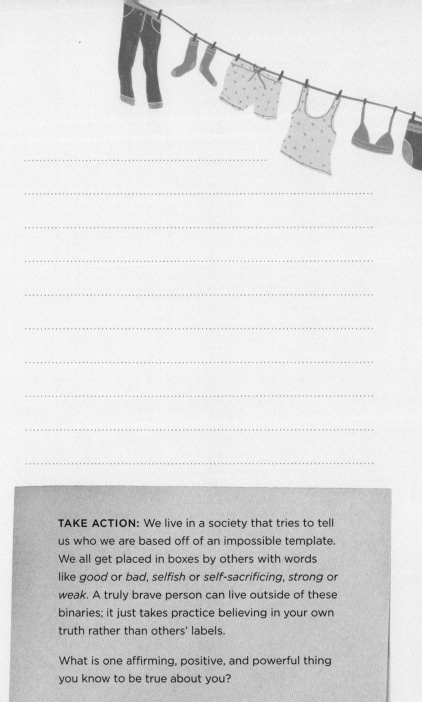

....

....

....

....

....

....

....

....

....

TAKE ACTION: We live in a society that tries to tell us who we are based off of an impossible template. We all get placed in boxes by others with words like *good* or *bad*, *selfish* or *self-sacrificing*, *strong* or *weak*. A truly brave person can live outside of these binaries; it just takes practice believing in your own truth rather than others' labels.

What is one affirming, positive, and powerful thing you know to be true about you?

....

We build our bravery muscles one act at a time, big or small.

—RESHMA SAUJANI,
BRAVE, NOT PERFECT

List 34

THIS WEEK, TAKE YOUR JOURNAL WITH YOU TO WORK,
MEETUPS WITH FRIENDS, AND BACK HOME SO YOU CAN
DOCUMENT LITTLE ACTS OF BRAVERY YOU SEE IN THE
PEOPLE AROUND YOU AND WITHIN YOURSELF.

....

....

....

....

....

....

....

....

....

....

TAKE ACTION: At the end of the week, reflect back on your list. Are you surprised at all the subtle ways you noticed yourself and others being confident and brave that you normally wouldn't have even taken the time to acknowledge?

List 35

LIST THE THINGS YOU HAVE STARTED
BUT NEVER FINISHED.

....

....

....

....

....

....

....

....

....

....

TAKE ACTION: Look at this list and circle the things that you feel bad about not finishing or that ended up going in a different direction than you expected. Think about releasing those feelings. Choosing to get upset that things aren't the way you wish they were doesn't serve you. It just sucks up your emotional energy and the valuable time you could be using to do something else! Scribble out all of the things that make you feel bad about yourself. Let it go.

List 36

LIST THE THINGS YOU WOULD TELL YOUR YOUNGER
SELF TO HELP THEM FACE THE CHALLENGES OR
SCARY THINGS IN THEIR LIFE.

....

....

....

....

....

....

....

....

....

....

....

TAKE ACTION: Take five minutes today to close your eyes and visualize the younger you who still lives within you. All of our former selves still exist within us and deserve to receive the love, healing, and guidance that the grown-up you holds today. In your five-minute meditation, visualize the younger you that still exists and tell them all of the things you wrote down in your list. You are your own greatest healer, helper, and advocate.

List 37

LIST THE THINGS, RIGHT IN THIS INSTANT, THAT YOU
KNOW YOU NEED TO DEAL WITH, BE IT A TASK OR
EMOTIONS, RELATIONSHIPS, ETC.

....

....

....

....

....

....

....

....

....

....

....

TAKE ACTION: These are probably your greatest stressors, today and this week, the things that weigh on your chest and distract you when you need to be present. Circle the biggest immediate challenge on your list, and underline the easiest thing to face. Which will you choose to tackle first?

List 38

LIST THE THINGS YOU HAVE DONE IN YOUR LIFE
THAT YOU ONCE COULDN'T IMAGINE YOU WOULD
EVER DO, ACHIEVE, OR EXPERIENCE.

....

....

....

....

....

....

....

....

....

....

....

....

TAKE ACTION: What is one big way you can let go of someone else's expectation of you so you can replace it with your own belief in yourself? Remove the restraints on your potential.

List 39

THINK ABOUT A TYPICAL DAY FOR YOU.
FILL IN THE LISTS BELOW:

EVERY DAY, I FACE THE CHALLENGE OF:

....

....

....

....

....

....

....

....

....

....

....

....

TAKE ACTION: Look back on this list when you're facing a bigger challenge to remind yourself of all the ways you problem-solve, push through, and rise to the occasion on a day-to-day basis. You are *so* capable.

AND EVERY DAY, I SHOW I AM BRAVE BY:

....

....

....

....

....

....

....

....

....

....

....

....

....

Rise Up

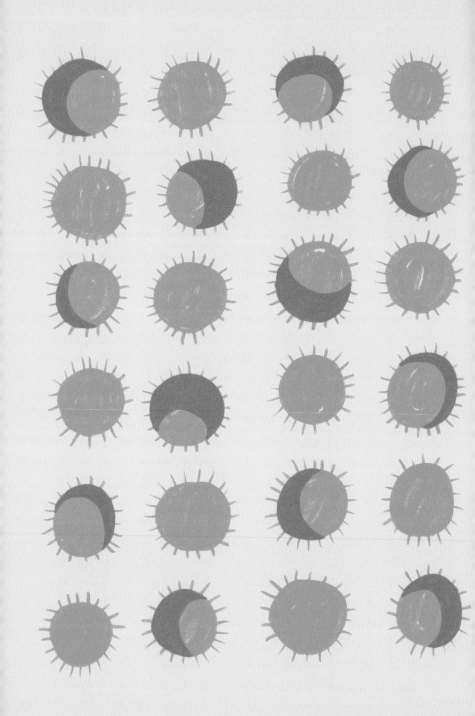

> Do not fear to be eccentric in opinion, for every opinion now accepted was once eccentric.
>
> —BERTRAND RUSSELL

When we can allow fear to exist in ourselves but not let it keep us from action, that is true bravery. Fear is perfectly normal, but sometimes it can hold you back from doing, expressing, or exploring something valuable to your life. Everybody experiences fear, even astronauts, even queens and kings, and even Beyoncé! But it is their push through fear that makes them people we look up to.

That nasty, gut churning, scary feeling can be a catalyst in your life, a physical and emotional motivator to just *do* something, to move forward instead of remaining stagnant. Just because something feels uncomfortable doesn't mean it's not good for you. The more you can trust that your fear is on your side, a resource and a guide, the more you can harness the power of your bravery each day.

You've dreamt of the person you want to be and the life you truly want to live. You have practiced dedicating time and thought to realizing your hopes and dreams. You've taken steps in your internal and external world to support and affirm your pursuit of bravery. And here we are, at the place where you embrace the authentic truth of who you are, what you want, and what you need and leap into the life you dream of. Bravery may feel nerve-racking sometimes, but you've already built a stable foundation on which to stand, and now is your time to rise up.

List 40

LIST THE LEAPS YOU HAVE TAKEN IN YOUR LIFE
WHERE YOU FACED AND OVERCAME FEAR.

....

....

....

....

....

....

....

....

....

....

TAKE ACTION: This is real, factual, actual data of your resilience! What does resilience mean? It means to know how to cope and keep going in spite of setbacks or limited resources. *Resilience* is a measure of how much you want something and how much you are willing, and able, to overcome obstacles to get it. How are the challenges you faced in the past valuable for your knowledge?

List 41

LIST THE CLOTHES/HAIRSTYLES/ACCESSORIES
YOU WEAR THAT MAKE YOU FEEL MORE
CONFIDENT, BOLD, AND CAPABLE.

···

···

···

···

···

···

···

TAKE ACTION: Build your armor. Everyone has certain tactile things that can be used as a source of empowerment and strength, whether it's a special necklace given to you by a relative or a colorful outfit that you feel bold in when you wear it. Look in your closet and decide what outfit is your armor of bravery. Wear it at least once this week and check in with how you feel at the end of your day.

List 42

LIST THE PEOPLE WHO MAKE YOU FEEL AT EASE
AND THE SPACES WHERE YOU CAN RELAX.

....

....

....

....

....

....

....

....

....

....

....

TAKE ACTION: We can't expect ourselves to be warriors of bravery every day. You are a multifaceted person who deserves a little rest and relaxation amidst your pursuits. And spending time with people who give us space to express ourselves is a good source of emotional rest. Take some time to rest your heart today, whether it's alone or with the people you feel very comfortable with.

List 43

LIST THE THINGS YOU WOULD SAY IF YOU WERE
SPEAKING YOUR TRUTH.

LIST WHAT YOU ASSUME MIGHT HAPPEN
IF YOU SPOKE THOSE TRUTHS.

☐ ....
....

☐ ....
....

☐ ....
....

☐ ....
....

☐ ....

TAKE ACTION: In the box next to each assumption, using a scale of 1 (not likely) to 10 (very likely), write the likelihood of your assumption coming true if you are truly open and honest. Know that when you take the risk of being open and honest with others, you gain power of influence. And no matter how they respond to your truth, by speaking openly and honestly, you are changing the world for good. Your risk, no matter the outcome, gains purpose.

List 44

LIST THE CONSEQUENCES OF *NOT* SPEAKING YOUR TRUTH
AND HOW THAT IMPACTS YOU OR OTHER PEOPLE.

....

....

....

....

....

....

....

....

....

....

....

....

TAKE ACTION: Does contemplating this list make you feel more motivated to speak bravely? Write down one thing you want to focus on expressing this month:

....

List 45

LIST THE WAYS YOU HAVE FORGIVEN OTHERS,
MOVED ON, AND LET GO.

....

....

....

....

....

....

....

....

....

....

....

....

....

....

....

....

....

....

....

....

....

....

....

....

TAKE ACTION: How many times do you think you have forgiven people and moved on to build a deeper connection? By being honest about your feelings, allowing others to process as well, forgiving them, and moving on together with a clearer understanding, deeper relationships grow. Your willingness to forgive without forgetting gives those you love the opportunity to build resilience alongside you.

List 46

LIST THE WAYS YOU HAVE FORGIVEN YOURSELF.

....

....

....

....

....

....

....

....

....

....

....

TAKE ACTION: Is it easier for you to forgive others or forgive yourself? A huge part of building resilience in yourself is to allow present you to forgive past you. You get to grow and change for the better. Equally, those around you deserve the chance to try again, do better, and be better. If you have an easier time forgiving others, think of how you love them next time you are criticizing yourself, and apply that love to you. You are your greatest friend and family.

List 47

LIST THE WAYS YOU FEEL ASSURED AND SECURE IN
WHO YOU ARE, WHERE YOU ARE, AND WHAT YOU
ASPIRE TOWARD.

....

....

....

....

....

....

....

....

....

....

....

....

TAKE ACTION: We can often confuse confidence and a sense of security with cockiness and pride. You feeling your best is not a problem; it's a gift to yourself and the world around you! Each morning this week, reread this list to remind yourself you are exactly where you need to be in this moment.

I learned that courage was not the absence of fear, but the triumph over it. The brave man is not he who does not feel afraid, but he who conquers that fear.

—NELSON MANDELA

List 48

LIST THE THINGS YOU HAVE SUCCEEDED AT AFTER
FAILING ONE TIME (OR MANY TIMES) BEFORE.

LIST THE THINGS THAT YOU WANT TO ACHIEVE NOW THAT YOU CAN PROBABLY DO BETTER BECAUSE OF WHAT YOU LEARNED FROM ATTEMPTING OR FAILING IN THE PAST.

....

....

....

....

....

....

....

....

TAKE ACTION: Circle one goal and give yourself a due date. Choose a friend or family member who can hold you accountable to follow through on your goal, checking in with you weekly until you complete it. And remember, the mistakes you have made in the past are what guide you to make better decisions this time around.

List 49

LIST THE WAYS YOU WANT TO CULTIVATE BRAVERY IN OTHERS BASED ON HOW YOU INTERACT WITH CLOSE FRIENDS, FAMILY, AND NEW PEOPLE YOU MEET.

....

....

....

....

....

....

TAKE ACTION: Bravery includes empathy—
the ability to see someone else's struggle,
to choose to relate to it, and to seek ways
to empower them in their own bravery. This
week, what is one small way you will use your
bravery to empower people you interact with
daily or weekly?

List 50

LIST THE THINGS YOU HAVE THE COURAGE TO
DO NOW THAT YOU DIDN'T BEFORE STARTING
THIS JOURNAL.

....

....

....

....

....

....

....

....

....

....

....

....

....

....

....

....

....

....

....

....

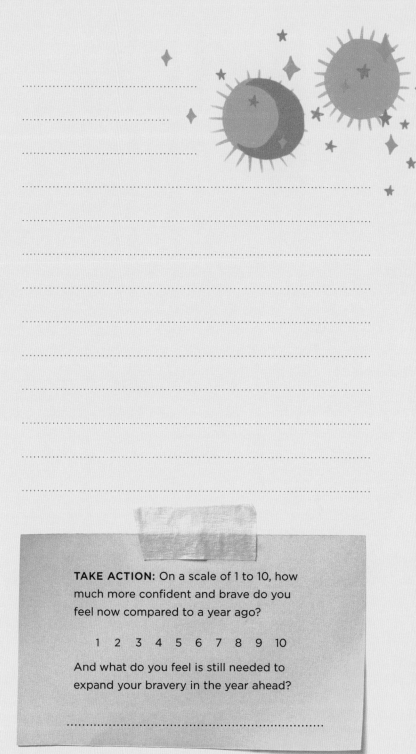

....
....
....
....
....
....
....
....
....
....
....

TAKE ACTION: On a scale of 1 to 10, how much more confident and brave do you feel now compared to a year ago?

1   2   3   4   5   6   7   8   9   10

And what do you feel is still needed to expand your bravery in the year ahead?

....

List 51

LIST THE TYPES OF ASSISTANCE AND EMPOWERMENT
YOU FEEL YOU CAN PROVIDE FOR YOUR GREATER
COMMUNITIES—LOCALLY, GLOBALLY, AND ONLINE—
BECAUSE OF YOUR GROWING BRAVERY.

....

....

....

....

....

....

....

....

....

....

TAKE ACTION: The power is in your hands and always has been. You are the only person holding you back from making a greater positive impact on the world! Make a commitment for the coming year.

I will use my bravery to impact the world by:

....

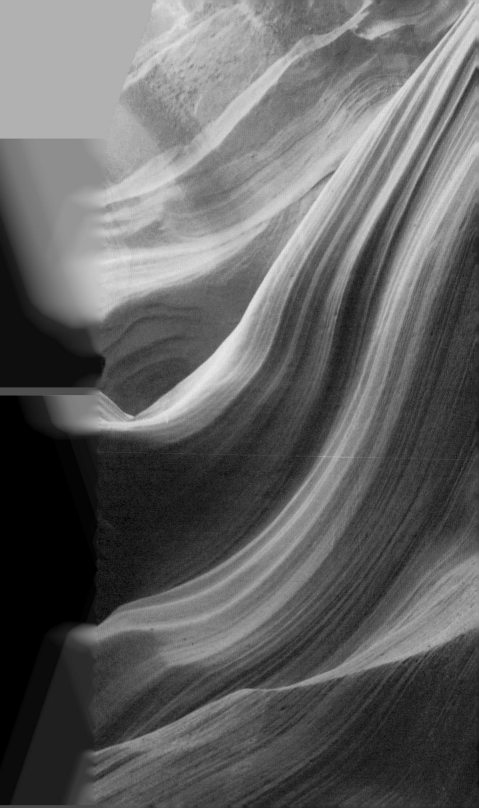

List 52

LIST THE VARIETY OF WAYS YOU HAVE BEEN BRAVE
THIS YEAR, BIG AND SMALL.

....

....

....

....

....

....

....

....

....

TAKE ACTION: You have so much to celebrate! Look at what you have achieved by trusting in yourself, looking fear in the face, and saying, "I can get through this." Fill out the certificate on the next page and post it somewhere where you can reference it daily, be it on your social media accounts or in your closet. Your bravery is never far away from you. It lives within. It may be quiet some days, but it's always there, waiting for you when you need it.

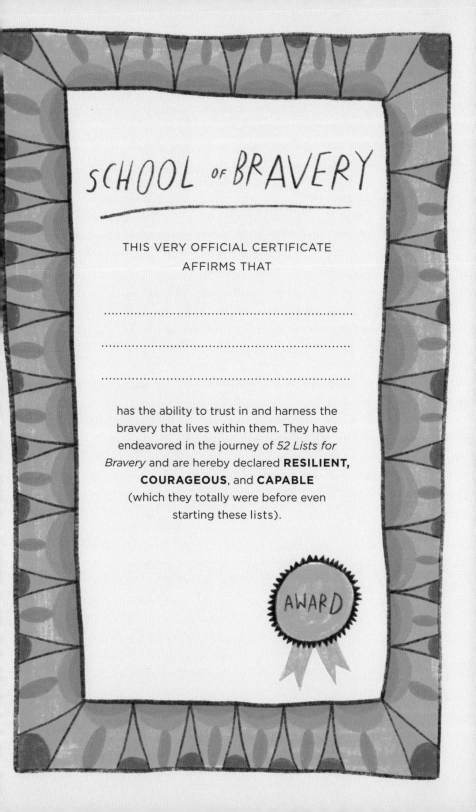

SCHOOL OF BRAVERY

THIS VERY OFFICIAL CERTIFICATE
AFFIRMS THAT

....

....

....

has the ability to trust in and harness the
bravery that lives within them. They have
endeavored in the journey of *52 Lists for
Bravery* and are hereby declared **RESILIENT,
COURAGEOUS**, and **CAPABLE**
(which they totally were before even
starting these lists).

AWARD

RESOURCES

- *Attached: The New Science of Adult Attachment and How It Can Help You Find—and Keep—Love* by Amir Levine and Rachel Heller

- *Avoidant: How to Love (or Leave) a Dismissive Partner* by Jeb Kinnison

- *Big Magic: Creative Living Beyond Fear* by Elizabeth Gilbert

- *Daring Greatly: How the Courage to Be Vulnerable Transforms the Way We Live, Love, Parent, and Lead* by Brené Brown

- *The Gifts of Imperfection: Let Go of Who You Think You're Supposed to Be and Embrace Who You Are* by Brené Brown

- *Love Warrior: A Memoir* by Glennon Doyle

- *More Than Enough: Claiming Space for Who You Are (No Matter What They Say)* by Elaine Welteroth

- *The Untethered Soul: The Journey Beyond Yourself* by Michael A. Singer

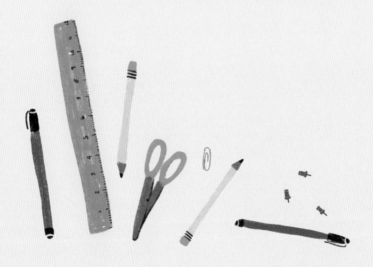

How to Find a Therapist

- The difference between a psychologist and a psychiatrist: Psychologists (a.k.a. therapists) focus extensively on treating their clients' emotional and mental suffering with talk and behavioral intervention. Psychiatrists, on the other hand, are medical professionals who spend much of their time prescribing medications for their clients and managing those medications as a course of treatment. I recommend first talking with a psychologist. Your psychologist can then recommend you to a psychiatrist if you need additional support.

- If you have insurance, your insurance provider should have a list of therapists that are within your network. Visit your provider's website or give them a call to obtain this list.

- Don't have insurance? That's OK! Go to OpenPathCollective .org to find a sliding-scale therapist in your area.

- Just need someone to talk to who feels safe? Check out one of these amazing organizations, some of which have 24/7 access to licensed counselors.

  - 7Cups.com
  - BetterHelp.com
  - Breakthrough.com
  - Talkspace.com

- You don't have to settle for the first therapist you visit! Try testing out three therapists, one session each, to see which one you vibe with best. It's kind of like dating or making friends—you have to find someone who really gets you. When you find a therapist who can challenge you to open up in ways that feel safe to you, it will make a world of difference.

- Do you have specific ways in which you want to grow in your confidence, inner security, bravery, and resilience? Most therapists specialize in multiple fields—like anxiety and panic disorders, substance abuse, eating disorders, marriage and family counseling, etc. Try the "Find a Therapist" feature on the Psychology Today website (PsychologyToday.com/us /therapists)—it makes it easy to search for specialties within a geographical area, and even by insurance plan. You can also search therapists by specialty in the "Find a Therapist Directory" on the website of the Anxiety and Depression Association of America: Members.ADAA.org/page/FATMain. For help worldwide, see InternationalTherapistDirectory.com.

- I recommend starting with cognitive behavioral therapy (CBT), the most common type of talk therapy, which can help you feel empowered to face the challenges of your life by improving the way you think and behave. Your cognitive behavioral therapist can refer you to other types of therapy if needed.

- Do you come from a cultural or religious background with specific needs? If so, there are therapists out there who can and will understand your unique value system, upbringing, and experiences. A great therapist will be neutral in their opinions on your background and beliefs, but it's totally okay to look for a therapist who will have a deeper understanding of where you're coming from on a cultural or religious level.

- I encourage you to work with therapists who welcome people of all races, religions, sexual orientations, gender identities and expressions, countries of origin, abilities, ethnicities, and body types. Their job is to help you explore and discover who you are and what you need to be well. And the more inclusive they are, the more opportunity there is for you to connect and heal.

MOOREA SEAL is a Seattle-based author, speaker, retailer, and designer, as well as an avid list maker with over one million books, journals, and stationery products in print. Her passion lies in giving voice to the inner child that lives within us all and providing resources for happiness, resilience, and self-expression. She finds hope in transparency and believes that to truly love and empower others, we must seek to accept and express our own true selves. Join her community at **MooreaSeal.com**.

SASQUATCH BOOKS with colophon is a registered trademark of Penguin Random House LLC

24 23 22 21 20   9 8 7 6 5 4 3 2 1

ISBN: 978-1-63217-331-7

Sasquatch Books • 1904 Third Avenue, Suite 710
Seattle, WA 98101
SasquatchBooks.com

Editor: Hannah Elnan • Production editor: Bridget Sweet • Design: Bryce de Flamand
Illustrations: Rani Ban • Illustrated type: Julia Manchik

Photo credits: Charity Burggraaf (cover), © iStock.com/Nikada (page 2), © Simon Matzinger (page 4), © Stephen Leonardi (pages 12–13), © Dejan Ristovski / Stocksy United (page 24), © Ryan Loughlin (page 27), © iStock.com/standret (pages 34–35), © Tatsuya Kanabe / Stocksy United (pages 42–43), © Ronald Cuyan (pages 48–49), © Gonz DDL (page 60), © Adam Nixon / Stocksy United (page 63), © Alexander Grabchilev / Stocksy United (pages 66–67), © Allie Smith (page 72), © Lucas Saugen / Stocksy United (page 75, 112–113), © Alejandro Moreno De Carlos / Stocksy United (pages 84–85), © Diane Villadsen / Stocksy United (pages 96–97), © Etienne Girardet (pages 104–105), © ILYA / Stocksy United (pages 120–121), © Scott Webb (pages 132–133), © Julia Volk / Stocksy United (pages 142–143), © Kevin Russ / Stocksy United (page 152)

Illustration on page 37 inspired by Maslow's Hierarchy of Needs